Abbreviations and Signs		Abreviaciones y Signos
W	Whole length of bow.	W	Todo el Arco
H	Half length of bow.	H	Mitad del Arco
lH	Lower half of bow.	lH	Mitad inferior del Arco
uH	Upper half of bow.	uH	Mitad superior del Arco
⅓	One-third of bow.	⅓	Un tercio de Arco
N	Nut of bow.	N	Talón (base del Arco)
M	Middle of bow.	M	En el medio
P	Point of bow.	P	En la punta del Arco
M*	In the middle, then at point, then at nut.	M*	En la mitad del Arco y de ahí hacia la punta ó hacia el talón (base del Arco)
⊓	Down-bow. (1)	⊓	Hacia abajo *)
V	Up-bow.	V	Hacia arriba
—	Broad detached stroke (détaché).(2)	—	Destacado largo **)
·	Staccato or martellato (martelé).	·	Staccato (picado) ó martellato (martillado)
ˌ	Thrown stroke (spiccato) or saltato (sautillé).	ˌ	Spiccato (brincado) ó Saltato (Saltillo)
)	Lift bow from string.	)	Levantar el Arco de las cuerdas

(1) When no sign appears at the beginning of an exercise, the first note is always to be taken at the nut with down-bow.

(2) Notes over which no sign for bowing is set, are to be played détaché.

*) De no hallarse ninguna señal al principio de un ejercicio, debe comenzarse siempre la primera nota en el talón con la arcada hacia abajo.

**) Cuando no se especifique la clase de golpe de arco, cada nota debe ser destacada.

Part I

Preparatory Exercises

No. 1

How to Hold the Bow

Practise the following with very short bows: (**a**) In the middle; (**b**) at the point; (**c**) at the nut. During the rests let the bow lie on the string while you count the beats aloud.

Parte I

Ejercicios Preparatorios

Nº 1

Como sostener el Arco

Trabájense los siguientes ejercicios con muy poca extensión de Arco: (**a**) en la mitad, (**b**) en la punta, (**c**) en el talón. Durante los silencios déjese descansar el Arco sobre las cuerdas y cuéntense los tiempos del compás en voz alta.

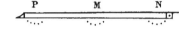

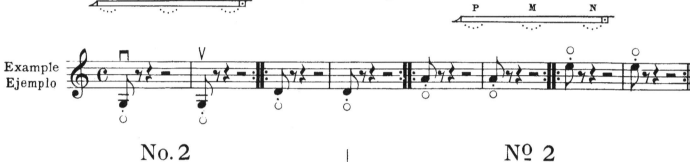

Example / Ejemplo

No. 2

How to Guide the Bow

Play the eighteen examples given below in six different ways, as shown:

Nº 2

Movimiento del Arco

Ejecútense los 18 ejemplos siguientes sin levantar el Arco, en las VI formas indicadas:

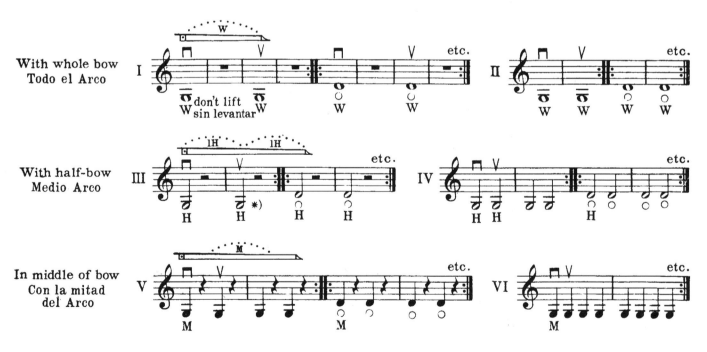

With whole bow / Todo el Arco

With half-bow / Medio Arco

In middle of bow / Con la mitad del Arco

*) First with lower half, then with upper half of the bow.

*) Primeramente con la mitad inferior y después con la mitad superior del Arco

Examples | Ejemplos

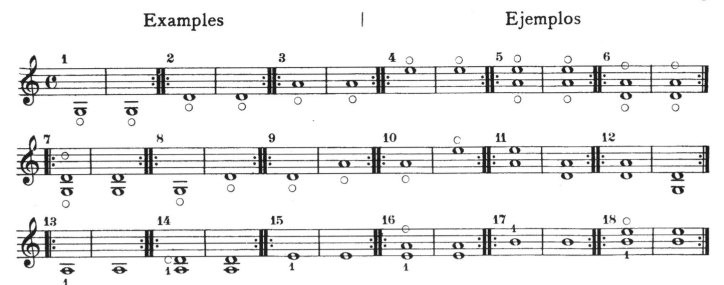

Rhythmic Exercises
Whole Bows and Subdivisions of Bow

No. 3

Example in Whole Notes
With 57 Variants

Practise each Variant of the given example from beginning to end of the latter.

Ejercicios rítmicos y división del Arco

Nº 3

Ejemplos en redondas
con 57 Variaciones

Estúdiese cada variación con todo el ejemplo.

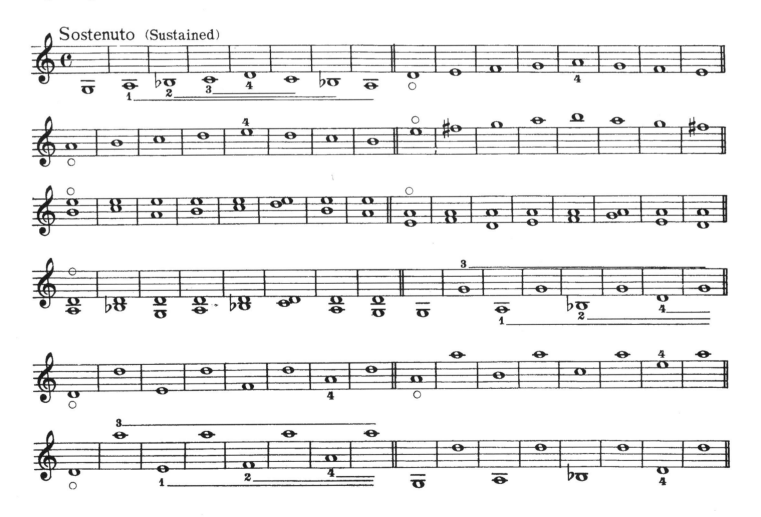

Variants
of the Preceding Example

Variaciones sobre
el ejemplo precedente

During the rests the bow must lie on the strings
Durante los silencios el Arco debe descansar sobre las cuerdas

(Metronome: ♩ = 66)

Whole bow
Todo el Arco

etc.

Each note with the up-bow
Cada nota con el Arco hacia arriba

Each note with the down-bow
Cada nota con el Arco hacia abajo

simile

(♩ = 50)

(♩ = 66)

Half-bows
Medio Arco

At first with lower half, then with upper half, of the bow
Primeramente con la mitad inferior, después con la mitad superior del Arco

With half-bows
and whole bows
Con la mitad y con
todo el Arco

In middle of bow *)
En la mitad
del Arco*)

With one-third
of the bow
Con la tercera
parte del Arco

a) N 1/3
b) M
c) P

No. 4
Study in Half-Notes
with 75 Variants

Nº 4
Estudio de blancas
con 75 Variaciones

The Détaché and Springing Bow

No.5 *)

Study in Quarter-notes
With 260 Variants

In order to develop the bowing in the high positions, practise each Variant also in the 6th Position. (See No. 8.)

Golpes de Arco destacados y saltados

Nº 5 *)

Estudio en negras
Con 260 Variaciones

Para el desarrollo del Arco en las posiciones superiores, debe practicarse también cada variación en la posicion 6ª (Véase Nº 8).

Variants | Variaciones

With very short bows
Con muy poca
extensión de Arco

With the wrist only
Con la muñeca
solamente

Syncopated legato notes
Ligaduras sincopadas

Dotted eighth-notes
Corcheas con puntillo

14

*) Together with the bowings from 136 to 260, bowings 1 to 109 in No. 6 should be practised.

*) Simultaneamente con los estudios de golpe de arco 136 - 260 deben trabajarse también los golpes de arco 1 - 109 del Nº 6.

Viotti's style of bowing
Golpe de Arco de Viotti

Preparatory exercise
Ejercicio preparatorio

The thrown stroke
Saltado

*) This mark) shows where the bow should be lifted for the first time.

* El signo) indica donde debe levantarse el Arco la primera vez.

No. 6

Study in Eighth-notes
With 214 Variants

For the same in the 7th Position, see No.10

Nº 6

Estudio en corcheas
con 214 cambios de Golpes de Arco

El mismo en la 7ª posición, véase Nº 10

Dotted eighth-notes
Corcheas con puntillo

Preparatory exercise
Ejercicio preparatorio

Syncopations
Síncopas

21

No.7

Study in Eighth-notes, in Six-Eight Time, with 91 Bowings

For the same in the 5th Position, see No.9.

Nº 7

Estudio en corcheas (compas $\frac{6}{8}$) con 91 cambios de golpes de Arco

El mismo en la 5ª posición, véase Nº 9.

Bowings
Golpes de Arco

Dotted eighth-notes
Corcheas con puntillo

Preparatory exercise
Ejercicio preparatorio

Employment
of the Foregoing Bowing-Exercises in the High Positions

No. 8
With the Bowings of No. 5
6th Position

Empleo de los Ejercicios
de Arco precedentes en las Posiciones superiores

Nº 8
Con los golpes de Arco del Nº 5
6ª Posición

6th Position
6ª Posición

No. 9
With the Bowings of No. 7
5th Position

Nº 9
Con los golpes de Arco del Nº 7
5ª Posición

5th Position
5ª Posición

IVª corda

2

No. 10
With the Bowings of No. 6
7th Position

Nº 10
Con los golpes de Arco del Nº 6
7ª Posición

7th Position / 7ª Posición

Exercises in Arpeggios over Three or Four Strings Employing the Preceding Bowing-Exercises
No. 11
With Bowings 1 to 198 in No. 6

Ejercicios de acordes arpegiados sobre 3 y 4 cuerdas, aplicándoseles los ejercicios de golpes de Arco precedentes
Nº 11
Con Golpes de Arco 1 a 198 en el Nº 6

1st Position / 1ª Posición

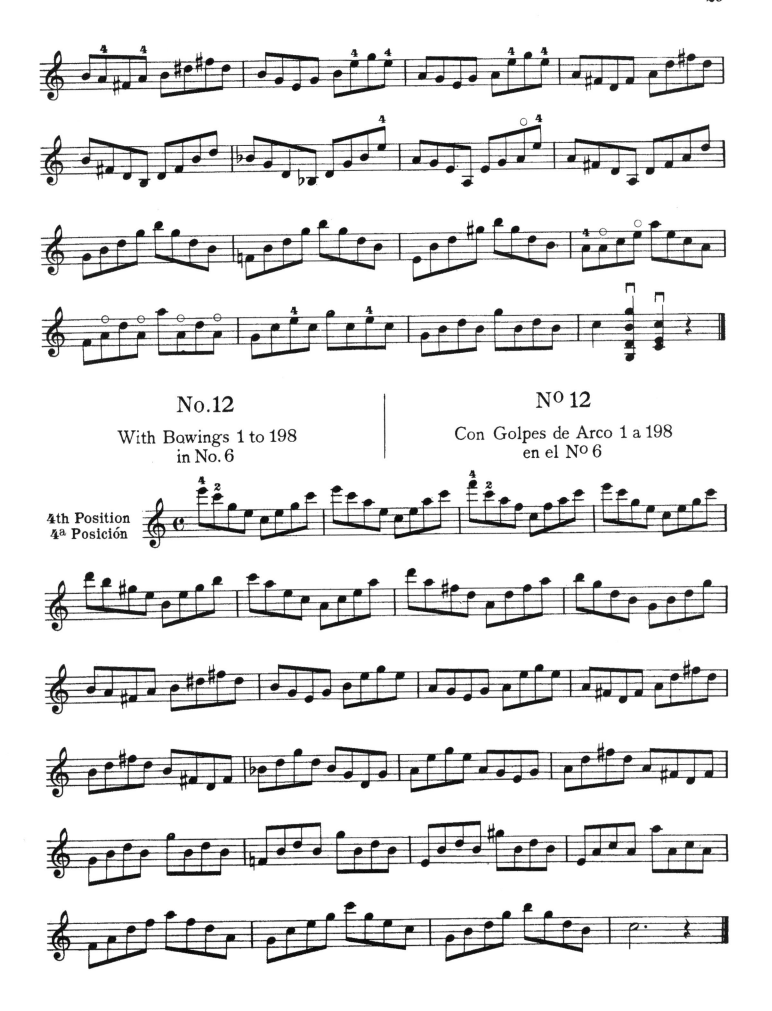

No. 12

With Bowings 1 to 198
in No. 6

N⁰ 12

Con Golpes de Arco 1 a 198
en el N⁰ 6

4th Position
4ª Posición

SCHIRMER'S LIBRARY OF MUSICAL CLASSICS

OTTAKAR ŠEVČÍK

Op. 2

The School of Bowing Technic

Escuela de la Técnica del Arco

Systematically and Progressively
Graded Bowing Exercises for the Violin

Preparatory exercises. Rhythmic exercises and dividing
of the bow-length. Detached and hopping styles of
bowing. Exercise in sustained tones and in economizing
the bow-length, i. e., holding it back as much as possible.

English Translations by
DR. THEODORE BAKER

Traducción española de
S. LOPEZ MIRANDA

⟶ Part I   Part II
Library Vol. 1182   Library Vol. 1183

Edited and Fingered by
PHILIPP MITTELL

G. SCHIRMER, Inc.

DISTRIBUTED BY

HAL•LEONARD®
CORPORATION
7777 W. BLUEMOUND RD. P.O. BOX 13819 MILWAUKEE, WI 53213